COLLINS LIVING HISTORY

MUGHAL AND BRITISH INDIA
1526-1800

Fiona Macdonald
Series editor: Christopher Culpin

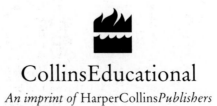

CollinsEducational
An imprint of HarperCollinsPublishers

Contents

attainment target 1

Questions aimed at this attainment target find out how much you know and understand about the past. Some questions are about how things were different in history: not only people's food, or clothes but their beliefs too. Others are about how things change through history, sometimes quickly, sometimes slowly, sometimes a little, sometimes a lot. Other questions ask you to explain why things were different in the past, and why changes took place.

attainment target 2

This attainment target is about understanding what people say about the past. Historians, as well as lots of other people, try to describe what the past was like. Sometimes they say different things. This attainment target is about understanding these differences and why they occur.

attainment target 3

This attainment target is about historical sources and how we use them to find out about the past. Some questions are about the historical evidence we can get from sources. Others ask you about how valuable this evidence might be.

Introduction

India is a vast and varied land, and the home of many different groups of people. Over the centuries, India and its people have seen the rise and fall of several great civilisations. Each has contributed, in its own way, to the development of present-day Indian life.

This book looks at just one of these magnificent past civilisations – the Mughal empire. Rulers from the Mughal dynasty governed a large part of India between the early 16th and the mid-19th centuries. However, it was long before the 1850s that the mighty Mughal empire began to weaken and a new, foreign power – the British – started to take its place. This book concentrates on the Mughal empire during its years of greatest glory, from 1526 to around 1800.

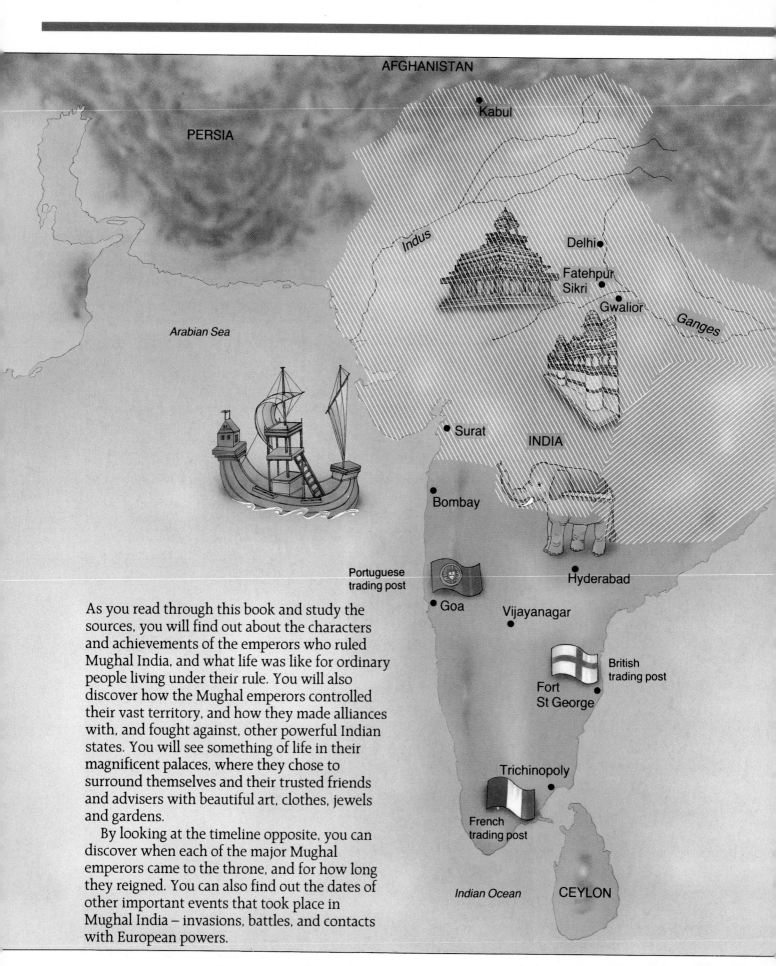

AFGHANISTAN

PERSIA

Kabul

Indus

Arabian Sea

Delhi

Fatehpur Sikri

Gwalior

Ganges

Surat

INDIA

Bombay

Portuguese trading post

Hyderabad

Goa

Vijayanagar

British trading post

Fort St George

Trichinopoly

French trading post

Indian Ocean

CEYLON

As you read through this book and study the sources, you will find out about the characters and achievements of the emperors who ruled Mughal India, and what life was like for ordinary people living under their rule. You will also discover how the Mughal emperors controlled their vast territory, and how they made alliances with, and fought against, other powerful Indian states. You will see something of life in their magnificent palaces, where they chose to surround themselves and their trusted friends and advisers with beautiful art, clothes, jewels and gardens.

By looking at the timeline opposite, you can discover when each of the major Mughal emperors came to the throne, and for how long they reigned. You can also find out the dates of other important events that took place in Mughal India – invasions, battles, and contacts with European powers.

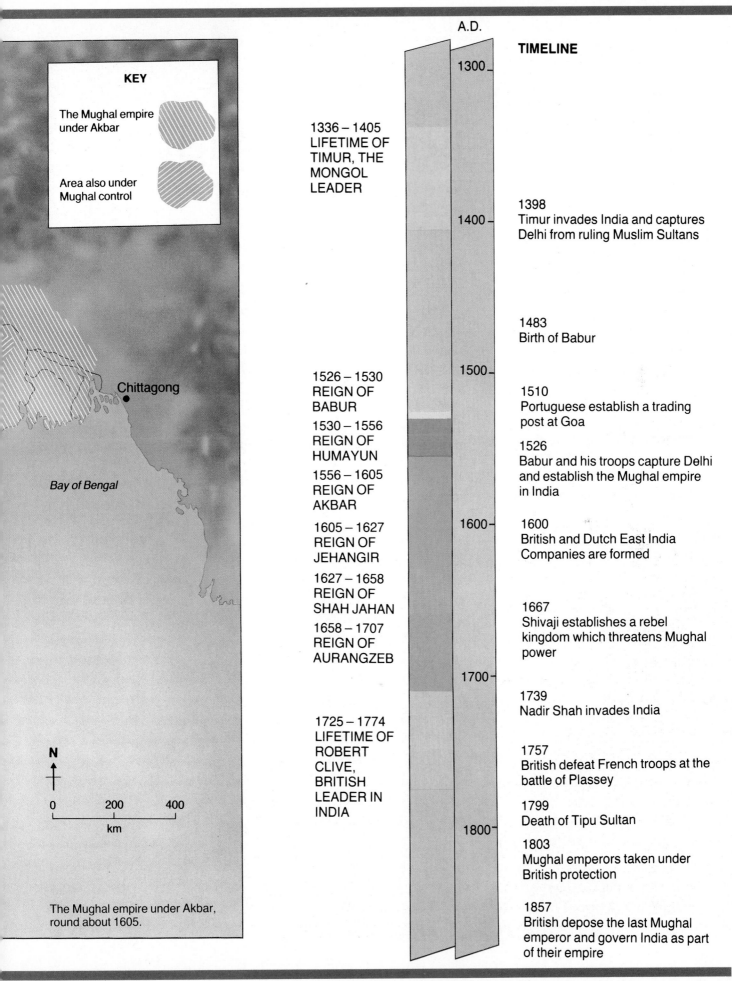

KEY

The Mughal empire under Akbar

Area also under Mughal control

Chittagong

Bay of Bengal

N

0   200   400
km

The Mughal empire under Akbar, round about 1605.

A.D.

1300

1400

1500

1600

1700

1800

1336 – 1405
LIFETIME OF
TIMUR, THE
MONGOL
LEADER

1526 – 1530
REIGN OF
BABUR

1530 – 1556
REIGN OF
HUMAYUN

1556 – 1605
REIGN OF
AKBAR

1605 – 1627
REIGN OF
JEHANGIR

1627 – 1658
REIGN OF
SHAH JAHAN

1658 – 1707
REIGN OF
AURANGZEB

1725 – 1774
LIFETIME OF
ROBERT
CLIVE,
BRITISH
LEADER IN
INDIA

TIMELINE

1398
Timur invades India and captures
Delhi from ruling Muslim Sultans

1483
Birth of Babur

1510
Portuguese establish a trading
post at Goa

1526
Babur and his troops capture Delhi
and establish the Mughal empire
in India

1600
British and Dutch East India
Companies are formed

1667
Shivaji establishes a rebel
kingdom which threatens Mughal
power

1739
Nadir Shah invades India

1757
British defeat French troops at the
battle of Plassey

1799
Death of Tipu Sultan

1803
Mughal emperors taken under
British protection

1857
British depose the last Mughal
emperor and govern India as part
of their empire

Before the Mughals

The Indian landscape

AIMS

Civilisation flourished in India long before the MUGHALS **seized power. The Mughals respected this civilisation, and used it to help them govern the country. In this unit we will look at India and at Indian civilisation before the Mughal invasion. What sort of land was it, and what was life like for the people who lived there?**

India is a vast and varied country. It is so big that it is often known as a SUB-CONTINENT. The Indian sub-continent stretches from the snowy Himalaya mountains in the north to palm-fringed tropical beaches in the south. In the west, there are the hot, dry deserts of Sind and Rajasthan. In the east are the damp, misty hillsides of Assam and the low-lying swamps of Bengal. Sources 1 and 3 show you how early travellers to India portrayed some of these different regions. They were fascinated by the beauty and variety of the scenery they saw. Source 2 shows a landscape painted by an Indian artist during the 18th century, and you can see the different types of Indian climate and countryside in Source 4.

Today, the Indian sub-continent is divided into several separate nations: India itself, Pakistan, Bangladesh, Nepal, Bhutan and Sri Lanka. In the past the land was often divided among different states. This was the situation the Mughals found when they first marched into India in 1513.

SOURCE 1
In the foothills of the Himalayas, at Gungotree. This was painted by a Scotsman, James Fraser, who visited the region in 1815.

SOURCE 2
This 18th century Indian painting shows the flat countryside of Bengal.

Invaders and travellers

Many of the Indian states were at war with one another. From the Mughals' point of view, this was a great advantage, because it meant that they would not suddenly become friends and join together to defeat the Mughal invasion. War had also weakened many of the Indian states, especially in the north of the country, and this made them easier to conquer.

In spite of these divisions and local conflicts, India was still a great prize for any invader. Travellers who had visited India before the Mughals came to power commented on the wisdom and justice of the local rulers, the richness of the countryside and the skills of the Indian people. You can see some examples of early descriptions of India in Sources 5 and 6. Marco Polo, who explored southern India round about the year 1300, believed that it was 'the most splendid PROVINCE in the world'.

SOURCE 3
A village in southern India, painted by an Englishman, William Prinsep, in 1820.

Motupalli . . . is ruled by a queen, who is a very wise woman. . . . I can tell you that throughout her forty years' reign she has governed her kingdom with a high standard of justice and fairness. . . . The people here . . . live on rice, meat, fish and fruit. The kingdom produces diamonds. . . . In this kingdom are made the best BUCKRAMS in the world. . . . There is no king or queen in the world who would not gladly wear a fabric with such delicacy and beauty. The country is well stocked with beasts . . . and with great abundance and variety of foodstuffs.

SOURCE 5
Marco Polo's description of one of the kingdoms of southern India. It was written round about 1300.

'The water, just freed from the ice, was piercing cold; and it required no small effort to stay long enough for the BRAHMIN to say the necessary prayers. . . . Afterwards, we entered the temple, where worship was performed, a little bell ringing all the time.'

SOURCE 6
A description of pilgrims bathing in the river shown in Source 1. It was written by James Fraser.

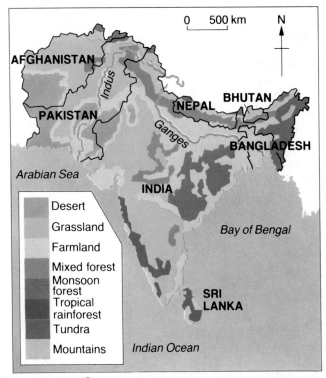

SOURCE 4
This map shows climate and vegetation in the Indian sub-continent and the present-day country names.

1 What evidence is there in these sources of the kinds of things produced by Indian civilisation?

2 What things mentioned in these sources would make India an attractive place to conquer?

Many people, one land

Like the Indian landscape and the Indian climate, the peoples of India were very varied. They had different languages, traditions, jobs, clothing and religions.

The most important religious groupings in India were HINDUS, MUSLIMS, BUDDHISTS, SIKHS, JAINS and PARSEES. There were also local divisions of these national faiths. The Hindu PHILOSOPHY divided people into CASTES, or groups, and Hindu society was organised according to these divisions. People usually lived next to, made friends with and married people of their own caste. They were careful to avoid close contact with the castes they felt to be 'beneath' them.

Each religion had its priests, or holy men: a group of Muslim holy men is shown in Source 7. Hindu priests were called BRAHMINS and they formed the most respected family groups in many villages. Some Hindu holy men chose to live outside everyday society and devoted themselves to philosophy and prayer. Buddhist monks, nuns and wandering scholars were also highly regarded for their learning and their disciplined way of life. Warriors were another powerful group in Indian society. Source 8 shows, for example, a group of Sikhs; some of them are armed with swords. Each faith also inspired its own art and architecture (see Source 9).

SOURCE 7
Muslim holy men in a garden. You can see, from their faces and from their different styles of clothing, that they come from many different parts of the Indian sub-continent. This picture was painted by a 17th century Indian artist.

SOURCE 8
One of the earliest-known portraits of a group of Sikhs, painted in the early 19th century.

SOURCE 9
This statue is from a Jain temple at Gwalior. Jain architecture flourished in northern and western India shortly before the Mughals came to power.

Traditional society

Yet, in many ways, life for the vast majority of Indian people was the same. Most people were villagers who made a living as farmers, craft workers or cattle-keepers. All these men and women spent their lives working hard to pay for food and shelter, caring for their families, and taking part in community life. You can see a picture of a typical Indian village, with men and women at work, in Source 10. In any case, as Sources 11 and 12 tell us, outsiders ignored many of the differences within Indian society, and admired the country and its people as a whole. As we can see from Source 13, traditional Indian society lasted for thousands of years because, like the rope made from many strands mentioned in that ancient text, it combined flexibility and usefulness with strength.

SOURCE 10

A village in Harayana, in north-western India. This picture was painted nearly 200 years ago. It shows a traditional way of life that was many centuries old.

'The Indians are naturally inclined to justice, and never depart from it in their actions. Their good faith, honesty and fidelity to their promises are known, and they are so famous for these qualities that people flock to their country from every side.'

SOURCE 11

A description of Indian people written by the medieval Muslim geographer, al-Idrisi.

'Public opinion is more powerful than the king, in the same way that a rope made of many fibres is strong enough to drag a lion.'

SOURCE 13

From the Shura Nitisara, a book about government written in India during the 10th century.

Indian women . . . have good stature (height), brown colour, and a plentiful share of beauty, with . . . a clear skin, fragrant breath, softness and grace, but old age comes quickly upon them. They are faithful and affectionate, very reliable, deep, sharp-tongued and of fine character. . . . They can master great things when compelled or provoked. Their women are good for childbirth, their men, for the protection of persons or property and for delicate handcrafts. They catch cold easily.

SOURCE 12

From a list compiled by an 11th century Arab slave-dealer.

> **attainment target 3**

1 Sources 11 and 12 describe Indian men and women as if they were all the same. Why is it unlikely that these descriptions are completely true?

2 Both these sources describe STEREOTYPES. Do such stereotypes have any use for historians?

3 What do Sources 11 and 12 tell us about:
  a India, and
  b the authors of these descriptions?

4 Which of the sources on pages 6 to 9 is the most useful for historians wanting to find out about:
  a the land of India, and
  b the people of India?

5 These four pages include sources of several types, for example, paintings, photographs and written sources. Which type of source do you find the most useful in beginning to understand what India was like?

SOURCE 15
Mongol soldiers on horseback shown on a decorative Persian plate from the 13th century.

Delhi is one of the most colourful cities. . . . Trumpeters and flute-players wait outside the doors of the Sultan's palace, ready to play a fanfare when anyone important arrives. Soldiers stand guard on raised platforms. Scribes make a note of anyone who enters the palace; they are watched over by the Keeper of the Register, who carries a gold mace and wears a jewelled tiara crowned with peacock feathers. . . . The Sultan receives visitors in the Hall of a Thousand Pillars. He sits cross-legged on a raised throne, with a large cushion supporting his back. He is attended by a servant with a fly-whisk, and by 200 armour-bearers carrying shields, swords and bows. Then 60 horses are led in, and arranged where the Sultan can see them. Next they bring in 50 elephants, decorated with silken cloths, their tusks shod with iron.

SOURCE 16
A description of the Sultan of Delhi's court, adapted from the memoirs of Ibn Battuta. He was a Muslim from north Africa who spent 20 years travelling in the East during the 14th century.

The Muslim lands

In 1398, Timur, the leader of the Mongol people, attacked Delhi and massacred its inhabitants. (The Mongols were NOMAD tribes who lived on the vast Central Asian plains, in present-day USSR and China.) Although Timur claimed to be a Muslim, he did not live like one. You can see pictures of Timur and Mongol soldiers in Sources 14 and 15. At the time of Timur's raids, Delhi was reported to be one of the finest cities in the world. You can read what one 14th century traveller wrote about it in Source 16.

The damage Timur caused in Delhi and the surrounding lands weakened the power of the SULTANS so much that it was fairly easy for another group of invaders, the Lodi Afghans, to seize control in the 15th century. As their name suggests, the Lodi DYNASTY originally came from Afghanistan, to the north-west of India. The Lodi chieftains conquered the once-powerful kingdom ruled by the Sultan of Delhi, and slowly extended their control.

SOURCE 17

The Jahaz Mahal (Ship Palace) at Mandu, in central India, built during the 15th century in Afghan style.

Building the Afghan empire

Like the earlier invaders of Delhi, the Lodi Afghans were Muslims. They built many fine MOSQUES, palaces, colleges and tombs in their new kingdom, using designs brought with them from Afghanistan, rather than the local Indian style. Source 17 shows a palace in Afghan style, built for another Afghan ruling dynasty.

On the eve of the Mughal invasions, various Afghan dynasties ruled over a large part of northern India. To the south of these territories, there were other Muslim states which were the remnants of the powerful Bahmani kingdom. This had once covered a large area in south-western India. You can see the extent of Muslim lands in Source 18.

When Babur, the first Mughal emperor, who also came from Central Asia, conquered Delhi in 1526, he was the third northern Muslim invader to attack the city in under 200 years. Babur was Timur's great-great-grandson and his wife was descended from another powerful Mongol leader, Genghis Khan. At first, Babur was not impressed with his new kingdom, as you can see from Source 19, but later he came to love the land and admire its people.

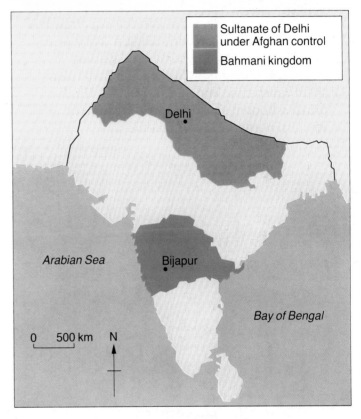

Sultanate of Delhi under Afghan control

Bahmani kingdom

Delhi

Arabian Sea

Bijapur

Bay of Bengal

0   500 km   N

SOURCE 18

Lands ruled by the Sultan of Delhi, the Afghans, and by the Bahmani kingdoms in the 15th century.

> Hindustan (north India) is a country that has few pleasures to recommend it. . . . The people . . . have no idea of the charms of friendly society, of frankly mixing together, of familiar conversation . . . they have no skill or knowledge in design or architecture . . . no horses, no good meat, no grapes or musk melons, no good fruits, no ice or cold water, no good food or bread, no baths.

SOURCE 19

A description of northern India, written by Babur, the first Mughal emperor, in his journal.

> **attainment target 2**

1 Look at Source 19. What does it tell us about Babur's homeland in Central Asia?

2 Do you think this source consists of facts, opinions or both? Give examples to support your answer.

3 How does Babur's description of India differ from Source 16, written by Ibn Battuta?

4 Which of the other sources here contradict or support Babur's descriptions of India?

The Hindu kingdoms

Most of the people living in India were followers of the Hindu faith, even though large parts of the country were governed by Muslims. Sometimes, Muslim rulers appointed capable Hindu officials to work for them and, over the years, a number of Hindus living in Muslim lands decided to adopt the Muslim faith.

Relations between Hindu and Muslim leaders were not so friendly, although their quarrels had almost nothing to do with religion. They were mostly about winning power and gaining territory. For example the Muslim Lodi rulers spent much time and energy fighting Hindu princes, known as Rajputs, who raided the western borders of their empire.

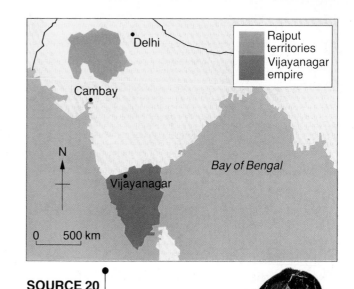

SOURCE 20
The Rajput kingdom and the Vijayanagar empire.

SOURCE 21
This palace at Gwalior was built for the Rajput leader Man Singh in the late 16th century.

SOURCE 22
This 17th century Indian painting shows Rajput troops defending a fortress.

The Rajput clans

The Rajput warriors lived in the desert kingdom of Rajasthan, which is shown in Source 20. Each Rajput prince was the leader of a group of families, or clans. The Rajput clans were fiercely loyal to their princes, but quarrelled bitterly among themselves and with neighbouring Muslim states. You can see a Rajput palace and Rajput troops in Sources 21 and 22.

The Vijayanagar empire

Further south was the mighty Vijayanagar empire. Its powerful and immensely wealthy Hindu kings governed a great city (also called Vijayanagar) with over half a million inhabitants, and ruled the surrounding lands. You can read a description of King Krishna Deva Raya of Vijayanagar in Source 23. We can perhaps imagine the former splendour of the city of Vijayanagar from the ruins shown in Source 24.

Travellers reported that the city of Vijayanagar measured over 11 kilometres from north to south, and that it had seven encircling city walls. The Vijayanagar empire controlled the thriving local cotton industry and the spice trade. This profitable trade linked India with the islands of the East Indies and with far-away Europe and the Middle East. Vijayanagar was destroyed in 1565 by Mughal troops, but written descriptions of it have survived. You can read extracts from these in Sources 25 and 26.

He is the most feared and perfect king that could possibly be, cheerful and very merry; he is one that seeks to honour foreigners, and receives them kindly, asking about all their business whatever their condition may be.

SOURCE 23
A description of the king of Vijayanagar, Krishna Deva Raya, written by a Portuguese traveller to India in 1522.

SOURCE 24
Ruins of one of the temples at Vijayanagar.

'It is as large as Rome and very beautiful to the sight. It has lakes and waterways and fruit gardens. . . . It is the best-provided city in the world . . . everything is plentiful. Rooms in the king's palace are decorated in ivory, carved with designs of roses and LOTUS FLOWERS . . . it is so rich and beautiful that you would hardly find another palace like it anywhere in the world.'

SOURCE 25
A description of the city of Vijayanagar by the same Portuguese traveller as in Source 23.

'The city is such that eye has not seen nor ear heard of any place resembling it upon the whole earth. . . . There are arcades and galleries to house the BAZAARS. . . . The royal palace is surrounded by many little rivers and streams, flowing through channels of cut stone, polished and even.'

SOURCE 26
Another description of Vijayanagar, by Abdur-Razzak, who travelled to India from Central Asia in about 1400.

1 Look at Source 21. Write down three words to describe the Rajput palace at Gwalior.

2 Why do you think the palace needed such strong walls?

3 Why do you think the outside walls, as well as the inside ones, are so richly decorated?

4 Why do you think the Mughals invaded India? Choose three or four sources from the whole of this unit to support your answer.

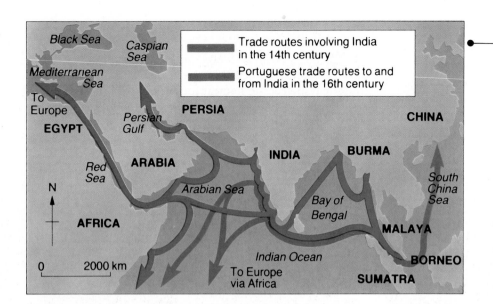

SOURCE 27
International trade routes to and from India.

SOURCE 28
Indian cloth was highly prized in Europe and elsewhere. This 16th century Indian painting shows weavers with bales of brilliantly-dyed silks and cottons.

Contacts with a wider world

Although it was the home of a rich and varied civilisation, India was also influenced by its contacts with other parts of the world. These contacts were made in many different ways. We have already seen, on pages 10 to 11, how the Afghan rulers brought their own style of architecture with them when they conquered the kingdoms of northern India. Earlier still, during the 11th century, the Islamic faith itself had been strengthened in that region as a result of Muslim conquests.

Trade and export

Trading contacts probably affected the largest number of Indian people. As you can see from Source 27, India was a meeting point for merchants travelling from many distant lands. Indian farmers grew the raw materials and craft workers made the finished goods that were exported from India. Sources 28, 29 and 30 show some of the many different kinds of merchandise for which India was famous.

'Imported from India: tigers, leopards, elephants, leopard skins, red rubies, white sandalwood, ebony and coconuts.'

SOURCE 30
From a list of Indian goods on sale in the great international market place in Baghdad during the 9th century.

About Malabar. . . . In this kingdom, there is great abundance of pepper and also of ginger, besides cinnamon in plenty and other spice, also coconuts. Buckrams are made here of the loveliest and most delicate texture in the world. Many other articles of merchandise are exported. In return, when merchants come here from overseas they load their ships with brass, cloth of gold and silk, SENDAL, gold, silver, cloves, SPIKENARD and other such spices that are not produced here in India.

About Gujarat . . . there is pepper here in profusion, also ginger and INDIGO. There is also plenty of cotton. . . . The manufactures of this kingdom include great quantities of leather goods, that is, the tanned hides of goats and buffalo, wild ox and other beasts. . . . They are exported to Africa and to many other countries.

SOURCE 29
From Marco Polo's *Travels*, written around 1300.

Religion and philosophy

Some travellers also brought religion with them, or made their journeys for religious reasons. Students and scholars from China came to India during the 6th to the 9th centuries to learn from the great scientists, mathematicians and philosophers who lived there. Indian Buddhist teachers travelled through the neighbouring lands, spreading the news of their faith. Muslim PILGRIMS from India made the journey to the holy city of Mecca, in Arabia. In the 16th century, Christian missionaries from Portugal and other parts of Europe came to India, to preach and to teach. Source 31 shows a painting of Portuguese ships by an Indian artist.

Cultural exchange

Indian artists were also influenced by other cultures. Beautiful objects from distant lands were carried back to India in the luggage of merchants and princes. Source 32 shows an example of Indian painting inspired by the brilliant Persian civilisation of the late 15th century. Later, in the 16th and 17th centuries, Mughal rulers invited Persian artists, poets and scholars to visit their courts to produce works of art. They also made alliances with the powerful Persian rulers.

SOURCE 31
An early 17th century painting of Portuguese ships by an Indian artist.

SOURCE 32
From the *Book of Delicacies*, a cookery book written and illustrated for the Sultan of Mandu, in central India, round about 1500. The Indian artists have copied typically Persian styles of drawing and painting.

ACTIVITY

Find at least three partners, and work together. Look at Sources 27–31. Imagine that some of you are Indian traders, another is a ship's master arriving in India with goods from overseas, one of you is an English merchant, making notes for a letter home to your master, and one of you is an African leather-dealer. You all meet on the quayside.

What questions do you ask one another about the goods you have to buy and sell? How do you fix a price for your bargains? How do you check the quality? How do you arrange to transport the goods you have brought? What stories do you have to tell about your adventures on your travels, or about the difficulties and dangers you encountered in getting hold of some of your merchandise? Act out your drama in front of other members of your class.

The Great Mughals

AIMS

In this unit we will look at the characters and achievements of the first six Mughal emperors, from Babur (who came to power in 1526) to Aurangzeb (who died in 1707). Together, they are often known as the 'Great Mughals'. We will also look at how the Mughal conquests, and the establishment of the Mughal empire, affected ordinary people living in towns and villages throughout India.

Babur conquers India

The first Mughal ruler to invade India was called Babur (Source 1). He was born in 1483, in the valley of Ferghana to the east of Samarkand in Central Asia. He was a descendant of the great Mongol leader Timur.

When he was only 14 years old, Babur led a successful raid to capture Samarkand, the Mongol capital, but his troops were unable to hold on to the city. In 1504 he managed to seize an important stronghold, Kabul in Afghanistan. He used this as a base from which to found his own empire, which is shown in Source 2. Before long, Babur began to plan raids towards the south. In 1523–1524 and again in 1525–1526, he led victorious campaigns to take over Delhi and to establish Mughal rule in India. Babur also defeated the Hindu Rajputs at the battle of Khanua in 1527, using typical Mughal fighting tactics (see Source 3). By 1530, Babur was in control of a large area in northern India. The Mughal dynasty had arrived.

SOURCE 1
Babur, the first Mughal emperor.

SOURCE 2
Babur's homeland and the territory he captured in northern India during the years 1523 to 1530.

Map labels: FERGHANA, Samarkand, KABUL, Kabul, Indus, Delhi, Ganges, Arabian Sea, 0 500 km, N

Approximate extent of Mughal empire at the time of Babur's death in 1530

SOURCE 3
Typical Mughal battle tactics. A SABAT is shown on the left and gunners on the right.

SOURCE 4
Humayun with his wife, Hamida, and his son, Akbar.

The reign of Humayun

Babur's son, Humayun, who is pictured in Source 4, was a less imposing figure than his father. Babur was brave, shrewd and capable of inspiring intense loyalty among his troops. He was also thoughtful, honest and sincere, as Source 5 reveals. By contrast, Humayun was elegant, but unstable and untrustworthy. He extended the Mughal lands south and west, but then lost all he had conquered, idling away a whole year 'taking his pleasure', according to Indian CHRONICLERS.

In 1537, the Mughal lands were attacked by Sher Khan Sur, an Afghan warrior prince, and Humayun was forced into exile in Persia. But in 1545, Sher Khan was killed by a cannon ball while besieging a fortress, and Humayun returned from exile to re-establish Mughal control. The last years of his reign were filled with fighting, against Indian princes and against his own brothers, who felt they could rule better. But Humayun managed to hold on to power until his death in 1556. He was supported, as Source 6 tells us, by self-seeking nobles, eager to win profitable positions.

'The truth should be reached in every matter, and every act should be recorded precisely as it occurred.'

SOURCE 5
This is an extract from Babur's memoirs.

> In very truth, the greater part of the inhabitants of this world are like a flock of sheep; wherever one goes, the others immediately follow.

SOURCE 6
One of the emperor's courtiers describes how Indian noble families flocked to support the Mughal emperors once it became clear that they had control of the land and its riches.

---

1 Make a list of the advantages that a sabat and guns might give to soldiers fighting against enemies armed with only swords or bows and arrows.

2 Make another list of the dangers that the sabat-builders and gunners faced.

Akbar

The Emperor Akbar was born in 1542, while his parents, Humayun and Hamida, were fleeing for their lives from Sher Khan and his troops. Great things were expected of the baby prince, as we can perhaps guess from Source 7. As Source 8 reveals, even as a young child, he was exceptionally brave and strong. Akbar was only 13 years old when his father died. At first he ruled with the help of a wise and trustworthy guardian, Bairam Khan. However when Akbar was 17, he dismissed Bairam and stayed in command of the Mughal empire for the next 46 years. He died, powerful and glorious, in 1605.

The pains of travail (childbirth) came upon Her Majesty (Hamida) and in that auspicious (happy) moment the unique pearl of the vice-regency of God (the baby Akbar) came forth in his glory . . . (he was then) bathed and made comfortable by the hands of shade-loving, radiance-darting, chaste (pure), rare-bodied nymphs (beautiful maidens) . . . (while) even-tempered, spiritually-minded nurses swathed the divine form and heavenly body in auspicious swaddling-bands (wrapped the baby in strips of cloth).

SOURCE 7
Description of Hamida giving birth to Akbar, the third Mughal emperor, written by one of his official BIOGRAPHERS.

SOURCE 8
Akbar wrestling with his cousin, when they were both small children. Akbar won the fight.

A successful military leader

Akbar is sometimes called 'the greatest of the Mughal emperors'. Why is this? There are several possible reasons to consider. First, he was a brilliant general: clever, decisive and swift to take action. He once led an army of 3,000 horsemen over 950 kilometres in only nine days, to make a surprise (and successful) attack on his enemies in the western province of Gujarat. He had an air of authority about him, as the pen portrait by his son tells us in Source 9. His officers and men were devoted to him, even though he could be ruthless. When he learned of a plot to murder his Prime Minister, he personally threw the ringleader over the palace balcony to his death. You can see a picture of this episode in Source 10.

'He was of middle height, of wheat-coloured complexion, with black eyes and eyebrows. His beauty was of form rather than of face, with a broad chest and long arms. . . . His voice was extremely loud, and in speaking or story-telling he was witty and lively. His whole air and appearance had little of the worldly, but instead revealed divine majesty.'

SOURCE 9
A description of Akbar by his son.

SOURCE 10

Akbar had to fight to become emperor. This 17th century painting shows him throwing the body of Adham Khan, his foster-brother, off a roof. Adham was cruel, deceitful and greedy. He wanted to seize power if he could. Akbar knew he was not safe while Adham Khan was still alive.

SOURCE 11

Akbar's troops fighting at the battle of Sarnal in the Punjab.

SOURCE 12

Akbar gives his reason for a lifetime spent fighting. From the AKBARNAMA, or history of Akbar's reign, written on his orders.

'A monarch should ever be intent on conquest, otherwise his neighbours rise in arms against him.'

Akbar increases his control

During his long reign, Akbar led his troops on many victorious campaigns. There is a picture of his army fighting in Source 11. He conquered Jaipur in 1569, Gujarat in 1572, Bengal in 1576, Kashmir in 1586, Orissa in 1592 and Sind in 1595. At the end of his reign, Akbar controlled nearly all of northern and central India, as well as lands in the north-west frontier provinces. The map on page 25 shows how much Akbar expanded the Mughal empire. His empire was varied and prosperous, but it was also rebellious and restless. The emperor could never afford to relax. You can read the reason which Akbar gave for spending most of his life fighting and putting down rebellions in Source 12.

Work with the rest of your class to discuss Source 7.

1 Listening to poetry and writing songs were favourite pastimes among the Mughals' courtiers. How does that explain why the writer used such extraordinary language to describe the birth of Prince Akbar?

2 What does this source tell us about how the Mughal emperors' courtiers behaved towards them?

3 This description was written when Akbar was an adult, and after he had become emperor. What other reasons can you think of for the writer's extravagant language?

4 The painting shown in Source 8, like Source 7, was produced after Akbar had become emperor. Why do you think it was painted?

Akbar's character

Akbar would be remembered as a great ruler, even if he had done nothing more than lead his army in the battles listed on pages 18 to 19. But he achieved very much more than that during his long years in power. Akbar was a remarkable character: energetic, forceful and terrifying. We can see this from the expression on the face of the captive brought before him in Source 13. Source 14 shows how he held court with great stateliness and magnificence, and Source 15 explains how Akbar made sure all the events of his court and empire were recorded.

SOURCE 13

This 17th century painting shows an enemy soldier captured and brought before Akbar.

SOURCE 14

Akbar receives a copy of the Akbarnama from Abdul-Fazl, his biographer. Akbar is seated on a throne, surrounded by his courtiers.

He has writers who by turns set down everything in writing which he does, so that there is nothing that happens in his lifetime which is not noted . . . not even his going to the necessary (lavatory) . . . and all that is done is with this purpose, that when he dies these writings of all his actions and speeches which are set down may be recorded in the chronicles (history books).

SOURCE 15

Comment by an English traveller in India who visited Akbar's court.

SOURCE 33
Tiger's claws like those used by Shivaji: a lethal hidden weapon.

SOURCE 32
The rebel leader Shivaji (1627–1680). A 17th century painting.

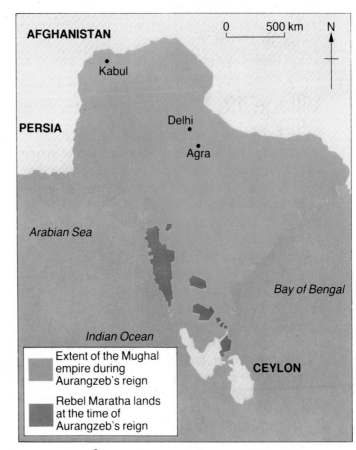

SOURCE 34
Mughal and rebel lands during Aurangzeb's reign.

Resistance from the Marathas

Aurangzeb's greatest opponents were the Marathas, a group of Hindu peoples who lived in central and southern India. They were fiercely independent and determined to resist Mughal rule. Their leader was Shivaji, a daring and ruthless chieftain, who used surprise raids and other terrorist tactics to capture important Mughal lands. You can see a picture of him in Source 32. Shivaji's most famous weapon was a set of steel blades which he fixed to his fingers, and which were known as 'tiger's claws'. They are pictured in Source 33. Aurangzeb never succeeded in defeating the Marathas, although he did win other important victories for the Mughals, as you can see from Source 34.

Aurangzeb died in 1707. Many historians consider him to be the last of the 'Great Mughals'. The Mughal dynasty continued to rule in India for another 150 years after his death, but it was never again so powerful. You can find out why the Mughal empire collapsed in unit 5.

---

1 How does Aurangzeb's behaviour contrast with what we know about other Mughal emperors' behaviour, and their attitude towards religion?

SOURCE 35
View of a village in the northern Indian province of Kashmir, painted in 1760.

SOURCE 36
Description of village life by a British visitor to India in 1830.

'The village communities are little republics having nearly everything they want within themselves; and almost independent of foreign relations. They seem to last when nothing else lasts. This union of the village communities, each one forming a little separate state in itself . . . is in a high degree conducive (linked) to their happiness, and to the enjoyment of a great degree of freedom and independence.'

SOURCE 37
A modern historian's comparison of life in India with life in Europe during the 17th and 18th centuries.

Village life

So far in this unit, we have looked at what life was like for the Mughal emperors, their courtiers and their officials. But what was life like for the ordinary men and women of India under Mughal rule? Source 35 shows a typical Indian village. If you look closely, you can see different activities going on: housework, farming, manufacturing, collecting water and firewood, and preparing food. Source 36 describes how a 19th century traveller felt about the villages he passed through. In some ways, he paints rather too cheerful a picture but in other ways he is quite right. Isolated villages often had little to do with the outside world, unless an army marched through their province or, like the Marathas, their local leaders called on them to revolt.

The impact of Mughal government

In some ways, the coming of the Mughals affected the ordinary people of India hardly at all. What mattered most to them was their families, their homes, their work, and being able to grow enough food for themselves and their animals. In contrast to the splendid Mughal emperors, they were miserably poor, but, as modern historians have pointed out (see Source 37), that was also true of ordinary people in other parts of the world.

There seems to be good ground for thinking that the average (Indian) peasant had more to eat than his European counterpart, and suffered no more oppression from the lords. . . . Most European travellers commented on the dire poverty of the (Indian countryside) but we must remember that . . . there was also dire poverty in the European countryside.

However, it is not true to say that the Mughal empire had no impact on ordinary people. Firstly, there was the Mughal system of taxation, which collected money from all farmers (Source 38) and from craft workers, like the cloth producers in Source 39. Sometimes these taxes were very heavy and left the villagers with hardly enough to live on.

Glossary

Akbarnama
A book which was written to record all the events of Akbar's reign.

Autobiography
The story of a person's life, written by themselves.

Bazaars
Markets.

Biographers
People who compile life histories or life stories.

Brahmins
People from the top rank in the *Hindu caste* system; originally families of priests.

Buckram
A fine cotton cloth.

Buddhists
People who follow the teachings of the religious leader known as the Buddha.

Calligraphy
Beautiful handwriting, you can see an example of *Mughal* calligraphy on page 36.

Carracks
Sailing ships, used to carry huge loads of cargo to Europe from India and elsewhere in the East.

Castes
The divisions within traditional *Hindu* society. There were four main castes – priests, warriors, merchants and farmers. There were also a group of people outside the caste system, known as 'untouchables'.

Chintz
Cloth printed with brightly coloured patterns.

Chroniclers
People who record events in the order that they happen.

Citrons
A fruit similar to a lemon

Diwan
Chief financial manager.

Dynasty
Ruling family.

Factories
Trading posts, offices and warehouses set up by the British East India Company in India.

Hindus
People who follow the Hindu religion and who worship the numerous Hindu gods.

Indigo
A plant used to make a deep blue dye. Cloths dyed with indigo blue were very popular in 17th-18th century Europe.

Jains
People who follow the Jain religion and lead simple, austere lives.

Joint stock companies
These were formed when a number of people joined together to lend money to finance trading activities. They shared the risks involved and also any profits that the companies made.

Kumiss
A drink, rather like yoghurt, which is made from fermented mare's milk.

Lotus flowers
The beautiful flowers of the lotus, a water-loving plant similar to the water-lily.

Manuscript
A document written by hand. *Mughal* manuscripts were often beautifully decorated with brilliant colours, gold leaf and pictures.

Marble
A smooth, white, valuable stone, used for statues and other precious objects, and on rare occasions, as in the Taj Mahal, for whole buildings.

Mosque
A building where *Muslims* meet to pray and listen to sermons.

Mughals
Members of the ruling *dynasty* founded by Babur. 'Mughal' is often used to describe the period from the 16th-18th century when the dynasty was most powerful in India.

Muslims
People who follow the faith of Islam and the example set by the Prophet Muhammad.

Nawab
Prince.

Nomads
People who live a wandering life.

Paradise
A beautiful place which *Muslims* believe will be the home after death of people who have lived good lives.

Parsees
People who follow the teachings of the religious leader Zoroaster, who lived in ancient Persia.

Pilgrims
People who make a journey for religious reasons, to visit a holy place.

Philosophy
A love of knowledge or wisdom; the search for truth.

Plantains
A fruit similar to the banana.

Poll-tax
A tax collected from all adult members of society. ('Poll' means 'head'.)

Province
Region or district.

Purdah
Keeping women hidden from public view.

Qur'an
A book, written in Arabic. *Muslims* believe that it contains God's message, revealed to the Prophet Muhammad, teaching people how to live.

Sabat
A deep tunnel hidden behind strong leather screens. Soldiers used sabats to give them some protection while advancing towards an enemy fortress.

Seal-engraving
Cutting beautiful designs into stones or jewels that were later to be used as seals. (In the days before everyone could read or write, seals were used to show that documents were genuine. The seal was pressed into a blob of hot wax, and the engraved design left an easily-recognisable pattern as the wax dried.)

Sendal
Fine silk cloth.

Sikhs
Followers of the Sikh religion, taught by Guru Nanak. (A 'Guru' is a wise and holy leader.)

Spikenard
A sweet-smelling perfume made from plants.

Standards
Flags or banners.

Stereotypes
Unreal (and sometimes unfair) descriptions of people based on half-truths, generalisations or opinions, rather than on fact. For example, one stereotype of teenagers describes them as all being noisy, rude, rebellious and scruffy.

Sub-continent
A small continent, or part of a continent.

Sultan
Ruler.

Turban
A head covering, made of finely folded and wrapped cloth, worn by Indian men. Today, it is often worn only by *Sikhs*, but in *Mughal* India, many other men wore turban-style hats, (look at some of the paintings in this book).

Yak
A large, hairy, horned animal, related to cows and buffaloes.

Index

Page numbers in **bold** refer to illustrations/captions

First published 1991 by CollinsEducational
77-85 Fulham Palace Road
Hammersmith
London W6 8JB

ISBN 0 00 327232-X

Cover designed by Glynis Edwards
Book designed by Peartree Design Associates
Series planning by Nicole Lagneau
Edited by Helen Mortimer
Picture research by Caroline Mitchell
Artwork and introductory map by Julia Osorno
Map artwork by VAP Publishing Services
Production by Ken Ruskin

Typeset by Dorchester Typesetting Group Ltd

Printed and bound by Stige-Arti Grafiche, Italy

Acknowledgements

Every effort has been made to contact the holders of copyright material but if any have been inadvertently overlooked the publishers will be pleased to make the necessary arrangements at the first opportunity.

Photographs The publishers would like to thank the following for permission to reproduce photographs on these pages:

T = top, B = bottom, R = right, C = centre, L = left

Ancient Art & Architecture Collection 8BL, 10B, 34; Bodleian Library, University of Oxford 18 & 42L (Ms Ouseley Add. 171 f.13v), 40L (Ms. Douce Or. c.4f.29), 47L (MS.Eng.Misc. e.1634, f.89v and 90r); Bridgeman Art Library/Cheltenham Art Gallery and Museums 48B; British Library/Oriental and India Office Collections 6T&B, 7T, 9, 10T, 14, 15B, 23TR&TL, 26L, 28, 29L, TR&BR, 31L, 33L, 36R, 43TL, 46R&L, 48T, 53, 54T, 55B, 56, 57R&L, 59R, 60; courtesy of the Trustees of the British Museum/Oriental Antiquities 8BR, 16, 24L, 27L, 37L&R, 39L, 38B, 43B/Coins and Medals 23BL; courtesy of the Trustees of the Chester Beatty Library, Dublin 20R, 44, 45R; R. H. N. Dashwood Esq. 54B; Werner Forman Archive 15T; courtesy of the Freer Gallery of Art, Smithsonian Institution, Washington DC 17B (accession number 39.57); Christina Gascoigne 11T, 12T; Robert Harding Picture Library 8T/Prince of Wales Museum, Bombay, 13, 35T, 35BR/Christina Gascoigne, 36L/Raza Library, Ranpur, 38R, 40R/His Highness the Maharaja of Ahvar, 41R/Victoria and Albert Museum; Howard Hodgkin, London 30, 48TR; The Kier Collection, Ham 21; Melanesia International Trust Company Limited 50B; courtesy of the Director, National Army Museum, London 52; National Maritime Museum 45L; National Portrait Gallery 51T; P&O Art and Memorabilia Collection 47R; Earl of Plymouth/ 'Country Life' 51B; Private Collection 31R; Rijksmuseum 49; The Board of Trustees of the Royal Armouries 27R; Royal Asiatic Society 48C, 59L; Victoria and Albert Museum 12B, 17T, 19L&R, 20L, 22, 24R, 26R, 32, 33R, 35BL, 39R, 42R, 58; York City Art Gallery 55R.

Cover Photograph: Christina Gascoigne

The author and publishers gratefully acknowledge the following publications from which written sources in this book are drawn:

Penguin Books Ltd for extracts from Marco Polo, *The Travels*, translated by Ronald Latham, Penguin Classics, 1958, © Ronald Latham, 1958; for extracts from Percival Spear, *A History of India*, Volume II, Penguin Books, Revised Edition, 1973, © Percival Spear, 1965, 1970; Hakluyt Society for an extract from Peter Mundy, *Travels in Europe and Asia*, edited by Sir Richard Temple, 1907-36; Oxford University Press for extracts from B. Lewis (ed.) *Islam from the Prophet Muhammad to the Capture of Constantinople*, Volume II, OUP (New York) 1987; Shri Rajiv Gandhi and the Jawaharlal Nehru Memorial Fund for extracts from J. Nehru, *The Discovery of India*, OUP (New Delhi) 1946, New Edition 1989; Royal Asiatic Society for extracts from the *Baburnama*, translated by Annette Beveridge, 1921; for an extract from the *Humayun-nama*, translated by Annette Beveridge, 1902.